A Numb Thumb

by Isabelle Minturn
illustrated by Valeria Cis

Practice Decodable 67

McGraw Hill Education

Bothell, WA • Chicago, IL • Columbus, OH • New York, NY

MHEonline.com

McGraw Hill Education

Send all inquiries to:
McGraw-Hill Education
8787 Orion Place
Columbus, OH 43240

ISBN: 978-0-02-144954-5
MHID: 0-02-144954-6

Printed in China.

8 9 10 11 12 DSS 27 26 25 24 23

Click! Click! Click! Kim's thumb clicked.

Kim did not see a single interesting show.

Kim's thumb felt numb. Click! Click! Click!

"Boring—birds on a limb!" she muttered.

Kim's thumb clicked and clicked.

Her limb felt numb. Her arm was getting tired!

Click! Click! Click! "Lambs and sheep!" cried Kim. Kim's thumb clicked a little more.

Kim's head felt numb! "This is dumb!" said Kim.
Kim climbed out of the chair.

Kim ran out and laced up her skates.

"I am glad. I am not numb!" Kim said as she skated away.